ADVANCED YO-YO TRICKS

If you really want to learn to yo,
you might want to master the basics covered in:

YOU CAN YO-YO!

by Bruce Weber
with Yo-Yo Master Dale Oliver

SCHOLASTIC INC.

New York   Toronto   London   Auckland   Sydney
Mexico City   New Delhi   Hong Kong

Cover illustration by Paul Colin, interior illustrations by Robert Roper,
design by Louise Bova, interior layout by Zeljka Majetic

ISBN 0-439-12933-8

12 11 10 9 8 7 6 5 4 3 2 1   9/9 0 1 2 3 4/0
Printed in the U.S.A.
First Scholastic printing, September 1999

For the world's most famous yo-yo, Yo-Yo Ma

Contents

ADVANCED YO-YO TRICKS

Introduction

I must admit that the world of yo is pretty amazing. When I wrote *You Can Yo-Yo!* early in 1998, I never thought about a sequel. But here it is — and for a very good reason. Within the first four months that it was on sale, *You Can Yo-Yo!* sold just about a million copies. That's a lot of books in any language.

I got letters from friends I hadn't heard from in years. Their kids had ordered the book from a Scholastic Book Club or brought it home from a Scholastic Book Fair. And when the kids told their folks how much they loved the book, the parents had to brag about being my friend. It was exciting stuff.

And then the orders began floating in from Australia. It turns out that yo-yo is a very hot sport there. Suddenly, the publisher began talking about translating the book into Spanish. Goodness, this was fun.

That's where the idea of this sequel started. Many of our readers, mostly young and a few older, wrote or phoned or e-mailed that they were ready to move on to harder tricks. So suddenly I was back in the yo-yo business.

In the year between the books, so much has happened. The number of yo-yo contests has increased tremendously. The number of yo-yo web sites has seemingly tripled. Some of the sites are among the Internet's most entertaining, complete with super graphics and cool music. Participation figures are all skyrocketing. Cities are competing to host the world championships: Honolulu grabbed the 1999 competition, and Tokyo was in the running for the year 2000 meeting.

How many yo-yos were sold this year? Nobody will swear to an answer. But even the guesstimates are staggering. I've heard numbers as high as 200,000,000 yo-yos. That seems hard to believe, but even half that would be enormous.

And with all the yo-yo hype, of course every major manufacturer has an entire line of yo-yos. They come in various sizes and designs. (Fortunately, the shape has, for the most part, remained round.) Companies compete for shelf space in all sorts of stores — kite stores, yo-yo stores, mall shops, sporting goods stores. And the yo-yos range in price from just a couple of bucks all the way up to about $150.

To find out the latest doings, I again turned to

the friends and acquaintances I made when writing *You Can Yo-Yo!* I found out that young Alex Garcia of Hawaii, one of the up-and-comers we identified in 1998, had gone on to become the national champion. I also found out that there are all sorts of competitors who will be battling Alex for national and world honors now and well into the future.

My pal Dale Oliver was there for me again. Dale maintains one office in San Francisco and another in the Dallas area and doesn't get to spend much time in either. He travels to one event or another nearly every week and to schools all over the nation presenting his Yo Yo Fun and Science of Spin program.

His company, Spintastics, runs a special kind of competition for new yo-yoers. They've identified 24 basic tricks and eight harder ones. When players complete these tricks, they can win special patches from the company. The patches clearly identify these young people as future champions. A patch can also be won by training other kids to do the tricks. And, Dale told me, young people in Europe will be able to win the patches beginning in the year 2000.

I also sought out other yo-yo leaders. I learned more about the technology that will continue the sport's development into the next century. Everyone in the sport believes that someday the best will compete for Olympic medals.

And then, of course, there are the tricks. I'll review some of the basics first and then move on to such important topics as advanced tricks, on-the-string tricks, two-handed play, and more. The good news is, you may have already learned much of what you'll need to know. (But we'll review just in case.) The more advanced tricks are frequently combinations of the simpler tricks. As Dale Oliver says, "The key is doing something perfectly once. Then do it twice. And so on."

Have fun, and remember the secret word: practice!

Technically Speaking . . .

It's important to make certain you're comfortable with your yo-yo. Fixed-axle yo-yos provide the best degree of control. Usually, they're the least expensive. Problem is, they won't sleep as long as the transaxle yo-yos — which makes it very difficult to do most of the advanced tricks in this book. The generally accepted record for spin with a fixed axle yo-yo is an amazing 51 seconds, held by former world champ Dale Oliver.

Transaxle yo-yos come in two types, sleeve bearing and ball bearing. Both types come apart with a twist, which makes it easy to replace parts and to unknot and replace strings.

In both types of transaxle yo-yos, the string does not spin around the axle directly. Instead, the string is attached to a ring that spins around the axle. This makes the yo-yo spin smoother and longer, because the area between the ring and the axle has minimal friction. Friction

transaxle

slows down a yo-yo, making it difficult to perform longer tricks.

With a sleeve-bearing model, the yo-yo spins on the sleeve bearing. With a ball-bearing model, the string is attached to the outside race of the ball bearing. Ball bearings have even less friction than sleeve bearings.

Until recently, major competitions banned the use of transaxle yo-yos. But at the 1999 National Championships, the American Yo-Yo Association changed the rules to allow the use of any type of yo-yo.

"Brain" yo-yo

Some yo-yos also feature automatic return. These yo-yos are often called "yo-yos with a brain," because the "Brain" tells the yo-yo when it's time to jerk back up. There's a special clutch inside the yo-yo that grabs the string at just the right second. This feature is especially useful for beginners. You don't have to think about the proper time to jerk the yo-yo back to your hand!

The string of your yo-yo is very important. Make sure you measure it carefully. With the yo-yo on the floor, you should cut the string just above your belly button. Tie a good slipknot at the top of the string and place the string over the first knuckle of your middle finger. Don't forget to replace your string whenever it gets worn-out or dirty.

The tension on the string is important, too. If you're doing sleeping tricks, you need a loose string. If you're doing looping tricks, you need a tight string. To loosen a string, let the yo-yo hang at the end of the string. Then, turn it counterclockwise a few times. To tighten the string, turn the yo-yo clockwise several times.

Getting to the Next Level

Dozens of different types of yo-yo tricks are used in competition today. And according to experts like Dale Oliver, players create new tricks all the time. "It's amazing what the young players are able to do," he says.

Maybe you've even made up some tricks of your own! That's cool, since creativity is definitely important. Most of the major competitions finish up with a three-minute freestyle performance, where competitors put together a routine of tricks — including some required moves. We'll tell you more about that later.

There are hundreds of standard tricks to learn, too. And once you've mastered the basics, you'll soon be ready to compete against the best. That's because many advanced tricks simply build on easier tricks you've already learned. Sometimes, learning a new skill just means putting old tricks together in a certain combination.

One good thing about yo-yoing is that there are *always* new tricks to learn. For example, as you move up the yo-yo ladder, you'll find more string tricks than before — these are tricks that involve the yo-yo jumping onto the middle of its string and spinning along the line, not on the end of it.

We're going to go over a bunch of string tricks, and the mounts we use to start them. In this book, you'll also learn some picture tricks, where the string is held in various patterns to form shapes. And then we'll go over two-handed tricks — the kind used most in competitions.

What comes after that? Believe it or not, it's off-the-string tricks, one of the latest advances in yo-yo play. You won't learn about them in this book — right now, they're strictly for experts — but by the time you've mastered the rest of these advanced yo-yo tricks you'll be ready to give them a try. It's amazing what great yo-yoers can do!

Review

Let's start with a review of the basics. The key to starting virtually every trick is either a good Power Throw or a Forward Pass.

Reviewing the **Power Throw**: Hold the yo-yo in your palm, facing toward you. Raise your elbow until the yo-yo is about at ear level. That's the "make a muscle" position. Then bring your hand down hard in front of you. Let go of the yo-yo over the tips of your fingers as you begin the downward motion. Stop your hand just above the waist and turn it over. Catch the yo-yo when it returns to your hand.

Reviewing the **Forward Pass**: Using the same basic hold, start with your arm behind your back, palm facing backward. Swing your arm forward as if you were throwing a bowling ball. Let go of the yo-yo as you flick your wrist. It should roll off your hand, fly out in front of you, and come back to your hand. Catch it with your palm up.

The **Breakaway** is another way of throwing the yo-yo. You start with your arm in the "make a muscle" pose off to the side. Then throw the yo-yo out sharply, straightening your elbow as you flick your wrist. The yo-yo will fly out and down and begin to sleep.

Swing your arm across the front of your body and toward the other shoulder. The yo-yo will cross in front of you and come up on the other side. Jerk it back to your hand, and you've completed a Breakaway.

Next, you might want to brush up on your loops, although you don't need to have them perfected for many of the tricks in this book. For an **Outside Loop**, start with the Forward Pass we just went over. When the yo-yo comes back to you, simply turn your hand and wrist sharply to the outside. You'll want to loop the yo-yo tightly so it will circle your hand *outside* your wrist. Another quick flick sends the yo-yo out for a second forward pass.

If you can do Outside Loops, **Inside Loops** should be no problem. They're exactly the same, except you flick your wrist to the inside, and the yo-yo loops *inside* your wrist.

The tricks covered in *You Can Yo-Yo!* (Scholastic, 1998) or other books of basic yo-yo tricks form the building blocks for most of the advanced moves. Though it is not necessary to know all the tricks covered in such books, it may be helpful to use *You Can Yo-Yo!* as a reference when learning these more advanced tricks.

Advanced Tricks

The key to performing longer routines is regeneration. What does that mean? Simply that the yo-yo doesn't stop and return to your hand — it keeps moving by shooting back out for the next trick. Let's say it's been sleeping and is starting to return to your hand. Instead of catching the yo-yo and ending the trick, you loop it around your hand and send it back to the end of the string. This gets the yo-yo spinning again.

One standard regeneration trick is **Warp Drive**, which is a combination of Around the World and an Inside Loop.

1. Throw a Forward Pass. As the yo-yo starts back to your hand, whip it past your hand and out again. That's the Inside Loop.

2. Then, as the yo-yo shoots forward again, take it into an Around the World by circling the *sleeping* yo-yo all the way around.

3. When the yo-yo returns, jerk it in and loop it around again. Try to do three Around the Worlds in a row!

Important: *Remember the yo-yo is briefly out of your line of sight during this trick, so make certain that no one is near you. It can be dangerous.*

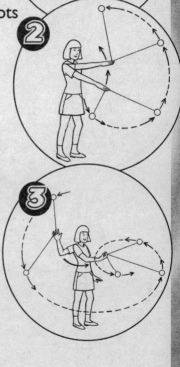

Once you've got Warp Drive, try a companion trick — **Time Warp**. This is actually a Reverse Warp Drive. It's another regeneration trick, combining Around the World, Hop the Fence, and Around the World Backward.

1. Start with an Around the World.

2. When the yo-yo completes the circle, do a Hop the Fence by jerking the yo-yo back, then hopping it over your hand so it rolls back down toward the ground.

3. Keep the momentum of the yo-yo going backward as you swing another Around the World circle in the opposite direction. Finally, jerk the yo-yo back to your hand.

Punching Bag is a variation of the Loops.

1. Force the yo-yo out instead of down as shown.

2. When the yo-yo returns, loop it around your wrist and shoot it back out again. Notice that the yo-yo is flying in the opposite direction as it does for the inside and outside loops.

3. Like a boxer in the gym, keep repeating as long as you can — or want to.

Vertical Loops is similar to Punching Bag. But this time instead of straight out, go for 90 degrees — straight up!

Caution:
Keep your eye on the yo-yo for these two tricks so it doesn't hit you in the face!

If you really want to show off for your friends, learn to do the **Bank Deposit**. It's not that hard, but it looks great.

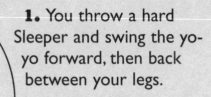

1. You throw a hard Sleeper and swing the yo-yo forward, then back between your legs.

2. With practice, the yo-yo will come up behind your leg, up your back, and wind up *in the pocket* of your off-hand side. While you're learning, it's a good idea to hold your pocket open with your thumb to provide a bigger target. And for goodness' sake, don't wear tight pants!

Note: *Your off hand is the hand not holding the yo-yo.*

Over the Falls is a relatively easy trick that will help you get comfortable with doing loops.

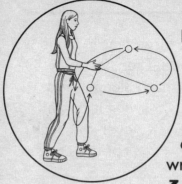

1. Start with the regular Forward Pass.

2. The yo-yo will come around your hand as if you were making a loop. But instead, push it *down* by twisting your wrist.

3. Now, catch it as it returns to your hand. Got it? Good.

The **Dog Bite** is another nifty trick that uses your pants as a prop. Here's how it works.

1. Throw a hard Sleeper and bring the yo-yo under your leg. Now, jerk it like you're bringing it back to your hand. But don't lift your hand, just jerk it.

2. If you get it right, the yo-yo will grab onto your pants like a pet who really loves you. For the best effect, try wearing lightweight, baggy pants.

Doing the **Elephant's Trunk** requires either a partner (with his or her arm extended) or a prop (a chair with an open back).

1. Place the chair about three feet in front of you. Then, throw a hard Sleeper and swing it up and over the back of the chair.

2. Allow the yo-yo to dangle so it looks like an elephant's trunk. Make sure it keeps spinning.

3. Finally, give a little jerk so the yo-yo will come back to your hand.

One of the reasons younger players are taking over the world of yo is their athletic ability.

You've got to have some to do the **Texas Cowboy**, which makes it look like you're an expert cattle roper.

1. Start by delivering a horizontal Around the World. You do this by using a side-arm delivery across your body to start a Sleeper. Get the yo-yo spinning about two feet off the floor. Now you're ready to dance! Lift your left leg and let the yo-yo approach and pass under it.

2. As the yo-yo continues in a circle, lift your right leg and let the yo-yo pass in front of you. End the trick by bringing the yo-yo back to your hand.

The more athletic players jump over the string with both feet at the same time. Yee-haw!

Next comes a trick that's perfect for fans of Mark McGwire and Sammy Sosa. It's called the **Homє Run**. You're standing on home plate. First base is just to your right. Second base is in front of you, and third is at your left.

1. Throw a hard Sleeper and move the yo-yo toward first base (about 45 degrees to your right) on an angle. Lower yourself down onto one knee. Gently lower the yo-yo to the ground at first base.

2. Move your arm from right to left so the yo-yo rolls in a semicircle around the bases. Finally, jerk it back to you at home plate, completing your yo-yo round-tripper.

Spaghetti is one of the few yo-yo tricks that requires sound effects. This time, the pasta comes in four-inch segments — of yo-yo string.

1. Throw a hard Sleeper and then use your off hand to pick up about four inches of string and place it into your yo-yo hand. Keep picking up string segments, about four inches at a time, until there isn't much left.

2. Bend down and make a giant slurping sound. At the exact same time, release the string, let the yo-yo drop down, and jerk it right back to your hand.

Note: *It is important to make sure that the back of your yo-yo hand is fully blocking your face so the yo-yo doesn't snap back up and hit you in the mouth.*

The **Sky Rocket** isn't for control freaks. This time the yo-yo is going to explode out of your hand and high into the air.

1. Throw a hard Sleeper, and carefully remove the loop from your yo-yo finger. Call the yo-yo back, and just before it reaches your hand, jerk the string, and let go.

2. The yo-yo will rise straight up. Be sure to catch it on the way down!

The top yo-yo pros can get the yo-yo to soar 35 to 40 feet in the air and catch it in their pocket. But be very careful — don't try that at home or any-where indoors.

It's often said that you can't teach an old dog new tricks. But a walking dog is another story. **Dog Through the Hoop** starts with the basic Walk the Dog.

1. Throw a Sleeper, then gently lower the yo-yo to the floor. But instead of walking it out in front of you, bring the "dog" behind your legs and then walk it through by letting the yo-yo roll along the ground.

2. Place your yo-yo hand on your hip to form the hoop and tug the string upward. Your well-trained "dog" will leap up from behind, through the hoop, and back down in front of you. A simple jerk, and your faithful companion will return to your hand.

Most subways run through a single city. But the next trick, **Through the Subway**, goes around the world. Actually it begins with a reverse Around the World.

1. Throw the yo-yo into the Sleeper position. But instead of throwing it straight down, use a sharp downward and backward motion. As you circle the yo-yo in a reverse Around the World, the "train" moves behind you, then over your head, and finally out front.

2. In the same motion, swing the yo-yo back between your legs (the subway tunnel), while bending forward at the waist. A quick jerk will bring the yo-yo creeping back through the tunnel to your hand. All aboard!

You need depth to learn the next trick. It's called **3-D**.... But 3-D only means that the yo-yo shoots out and away during the trick.

1. As usual, start with a good Sleeper. Then, with the thumb and index finger of your off hand, grab the string about a third of the way down.

2. Next, take the thumb and index finger of your yo-yo hand and grab the string another six inches below your off hand. Pull your yo-yo hand up. The yo-yo string should be hanging down from the thumb and index finger of your yo-yo hand.

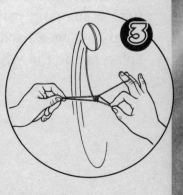

3. Now, swing the yo-yo out, then over the top and toward you, wrapping it two or three times around the two strings. On the final circle, let go, and shoot all of the string out. With practice, you can catch the yo-yo as it comes back to you.

Picture Tricks

If you've gotten this far, chances are you're well on your way to becoming a first-class yo-yoer! You've learned enough tricks to perform the compulsories in almost any competition. And you're probably good enough to wow every one of your friends. Congratulations!

What? You want to impress them even more? You need a whole new set of cool-looking tricks, harder than almost everything you've done so far. Picture tricks got their name because, when you perform them, the yo-yo string forms a picture in your hands. Are you ready? Let's start.

To master the tricks in this section you should practice first with a dead yo-yo — one that is not spinning. Once you've figured out how to handle the string, you can go to live practice with a spinning yo-yo. Just make sure you begin by throwing a hard sleeper so the yo-yo keeps spinning for the whole trick.

First, try the **Texas Star**. At the end, your string will look like a five-pointed star — the symbol of the Lone Star State.

1. Put the inside of the thumb of your off hand (the one without the yo-yo) onto the side of the string, about six inches from your yo-yo hand. Lift your off hand so the string forms a horizontal line in front of you, parallel to the ground.

Next, loop the outside of the string around the ring finger of your yo-yo hand, another few inches down. Pull that string so it, too, is parallel to the ground. The yo-yo should hang down in front of the parallel strings.

2. Then, take the index finger of your off hand and put the backside of that finger against the inside of the string, another six inches down. Lift this part of the string above and in front of the first two strings.

3. Still with us? Using the backside of the thumb of your yo-yo hand, reach between the two parallel strings, and pull through another section of the hanging string. You're almost there.

4. Take the backside of your yo-yo finger on your yo-yo hand and lift up the hanging string. You should now have the five points that make up the Texas star. The remaining string should be hanging down from the top center point, off your yo-yo finger.

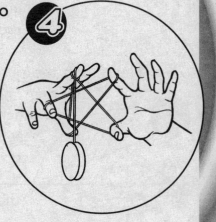

That's it. Finally, release all of your fingers, and let the yo-yo fall to the bottom. If you formed the star correctly, the string won't tangle at all. When you use a live yo-yo, the final step is to jerk it back to your hand. This is hard to do, but it's worth working for!

Once you master the Texas Star with a live yo-yo, you'll be ready to move on to the **Shooting Star**.

1. Start by making a Texas Star. When you've got all five points under control, the yo-yo will be dangling down from the top point.

2. Now, instead of releasing the yo-yo, swing it toward you and over the top. Do two or three swings, wrapping the yo-yo around the star.

3. When the yo-yo comes toward you the last time, release the entire star, and shoot the yo-yo out front as in a forward pass. The yo-yo will then fly back toward you. Be ready to catch it. Way to go!

One-handed Star looks like a smaller version of the Texas Star. Again, it's best to practice with a dead yo-yo.

1. Place the outside of your pinky (remember, you're only using your yo-yo hand) against the inside of the string (which faces you), about three inches from the top. Use that pinky to lift the string upward.

2. Reach down again, and using your index finger, loop the string around it. Now lift that finger (and the string) back up.

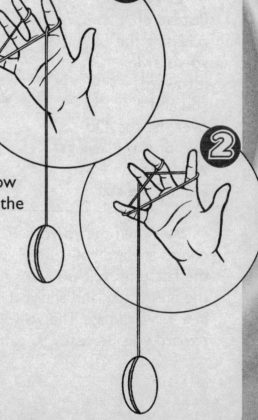

3. Then, take your ring finger, and put it against the inside of the string, again about three inches down. And again, lift up the string. Next, reach around the string with your thumb another three inches down.

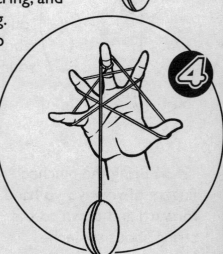

4. Finally, bring your middle finger around to the inside of the string, and again, lift up the string. Adjust your fingers so the string forms a small five-pointed star.

Once you can get your fingers moving fast enough, try it with the yo-yo spinning!

Ready for another picture trick? Try the **Bow Tie**.

1. With the yo-yo sleeping, pinch your thumbs and middle fingers together on both hands.

2. Place the pinched fingers of your off hand on the outside of the string about six inches below your yo-yo hand.

3. Bring the pinched fingers of your yo-yo hand forward and down to the string about six inches below your off hand.

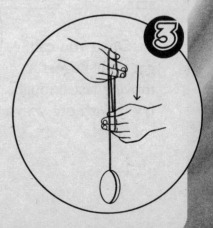

4. Bring your off hand forward and down below your yo-yo hand again. Grab the hanging string with the middle finger of your off hand.

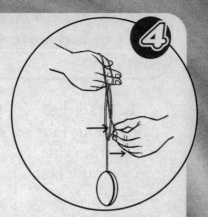

5. Drop the string from your off thumb. Reinsert your off thumb back into the loop the same direction with your off-hand middle finger.

6. Rotate both hands down and out, forming a bow tie! The yo-yo should hang from the center of the Bow Tie.

Release the string and jerk the yo-yo back to your hand to complete the trick.

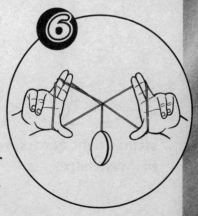

Now you can do another picture trick called the **Confederate Flag**. Practice this with a dead yo-yo.

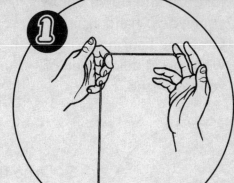

1. Grab the string about four inches from the top with the first three fingers of your off hand.

2. Skip down another four inches and grab the string again with the index, middle, and ring fingers of your yo-yo hand. When you pull the strings tight across, you'll have a triangle. You're halfway there.

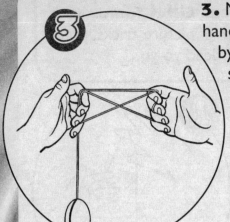

3. Next, using your off hand, repeat the first step by grabbing the hanging string with the first three fingers again. This will give you an X with a horizontal string on top.

4. Finally, use your yo-yo hand's pinky to grab the hanging string again. Pull the string across to form the bottom of the flag. That's it!

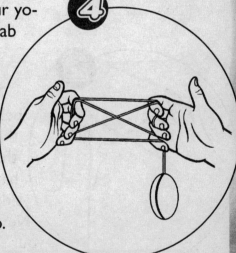

Now try the Confederate Flag with a spinning yo-yo.

Have you ever been to Paris? Why bother? You can make the famous **Eiffel Tower** with your yo-yo! Like the other picture tricks, practice this one first with a dead yo-yo.

1. Begin by looping the string over the thumb and index finger of your off hand and pull the string over and down, behind these fingers.

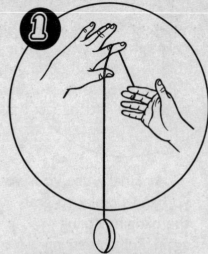

2. About four inches below this point, place the outside of the thumb of your yo-yo hand against the outside of the string. Next, twist the wrist of your off hand a half turn, forming an X in the loop.

3. Then, lower your off hand and grab the string with your thumb and index finger.

Let go of the loop as you pull the string through it with your thumb and index finger. Allow the loop to slide down the string as you lift your off hand upward.

4. Finally, make a cutting motion with the index and middle fingers of your yo-yo hand, palm up. "Cut" the hanging string so it pinches between your fingers. Now, move your fingers so your off hand is straight above your yo-yo hand, and tighten the string into the shape of the Eiffel Tower.

Once you get the idea, try it with a spinning yo-yo.

Doing an upside-down Eiffel Tower will start you on the next trick. It's called **Just Spell Yo**.

The upside-down tower will give you the letter Y. And as the yo-yo hangs down off your yo-yo hand, the round toy forms the letter O. See it? Now, swing the yo-yo O to the other side of the Y so your audience can see it, too. Yo! Yo!

Mounts

In a string trick, the yo-yo actually spins *on* the string — not just at the end of it! These tricks are lots of fun, and they look great to your friends and fans. But they're also hard and take lots of practice. You actually send the yo-yo flying out and/or up and then land it back on the extended string.

Hint: It's best to use a butterfly yo-yo for string tricks. It offers a better target for the string.

Every string trick begins with a mount. This simply means getting the yo-yo onto the string. There are five different mounts you can learn — front mount, side mount, split side mount, bottom mount, split bottom mount.

Which one you use depends upon the trick you choose. The famous Stop and Go starts with a front mount. The Side Barrel Roll starts with a split side mount. We'll show you how to do string tricks like these, but first you'll need to learn the mounts that start the tricks.

Mount #1: Front

The **Front Mount** is the most basic way to get the yo-yo onto the string.

1. Throw a hard Sleeper and put your off-hand index finger behind the string, about halfway down. Move your yo-yo hand down behind your off hand, draping the string over your extended index finger.

2. With the yo-yo hand, guide the string into the groove of the yo-yo.

3. Finally, lift your yo-yo hand up in front so that the spinning yo-yo is sitting on the string.

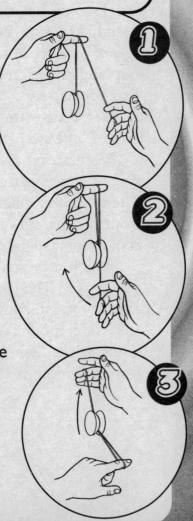

Now, let's use the mount you just learned to do a whole trick! In **Stop and Go**, the yo-yo actually comes to a full stop, then starts again.

1. Do a Front Mount.

2. Bring both hands together with the yo-yo hanging below, riding the string.

3. An upward jerk with your yo-yo hand will wrap all three strings around the yo-yo and bring it up into your hands.

4. The yo-yo is now stopped.

5. Pull your yo-yo hand down while the string rests on the index finger of your off hand. That's all it will take to get the yo-yo spinning again. Finally, pop it back into your hand.

Mount #2: Side

Next comes the **Side Mount**. This mount is also a trick, sometimes called the **Man on the Flying Trapeze**.

1. Throw a Breakaway.

2. As the yo-yo swings down, extend your off-hand index finger so that the string wraps around it.

3. With practice, the yo-yo should land on the extended string about four or five inches from your finger.

You're probably learning that in the world of yo usually the more complicated a trick is, the better. Take the Man on the Flying Trapeze, for instance. Some say that the **Triple Trapeze** is three times better!

1. Start a Triple Trapeze with a Side Mount.

2. After you have the yo-yo spinning on the string, lift and pull the off hand out of the string so the yo-yo pops up.

3. Normally, it would return to your hand, but for a Triple Trapeze, instead of catching it, you snap the yo-yo around your hand in an Outside Loop, as shown. This regenerates the spin so you can try for a second Man on the Flying Trapeze.

Repeat the motion once again, and you've got the Triple! This is a hard trick and takes lots of practice.

Mount #3: Split Side

Once you've learned the side mount, try the **Split Side Mount**.

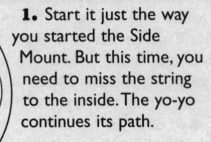

1. Start it just the way you started the Side Mount. But this time, you need to miss the string to the inside. The yo-yo continues its path.

2. Now, move the index finger of your yo-yo hand into the path of the swinging yo-yo, just above the yo-yo. For righties, this will mean that you put your yo-yo hand on the left side of the string, and for lefties, on the right side.

3. Make sure the yo-yo continues in the same direction (clockwise for righties, counterclockwise for lefties) and swing the yo-yo around that finger.

4. It should land on the string.

Once you've got the mount, how about a fast-action trick — the **Side Barrel Roll**. Of course, it begins with the Split Side Mount you just learned.

1. Once you get the yo-yo on the string, your hands will basically follow each other in a circle, making the yo-yo pass from one string to the other, within the loop.

2. To do this, take your off-hand index finger and pass it under the yo-yo.

3. Follow with your yo-yo hand index finger, in the same direction.

How can you score yourself on this one? Two rolls are good; more than two is even better!

Mount #4: Bottom

This one's a little tricky! For a **Bottom Mount**, you once again begin with a hard Sleeper.

1. Then you extend the index finger on your off hand in back of the string, as you did in the front mount. Only this time, you place your finger much closer to the yo-yo.

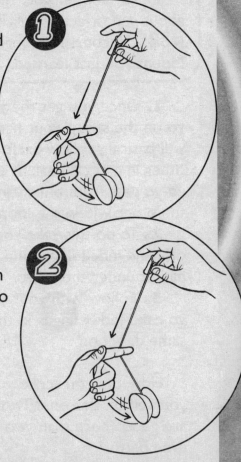

2. Loop the yo-yo around that finger from front to back (the yo-yo swings toward you). With practice, the yo-yo will land on the string.

3. Bring up your off hand so the yo-yo stays balanced.

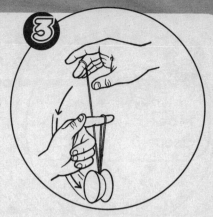

After you've learned this mount, you can wow your friends with **Bottom Mount Brain Twister** with front and back somersaults.

1. Start with the Bottom Mount.

2. Once you have the yo-yo on the string, pull the extended index finger of your off hand up above your yo-yo hand.

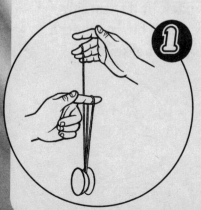
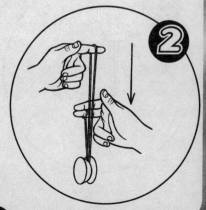

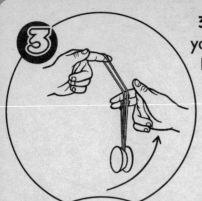

3. Now, move your yo-yo hand toward your body.

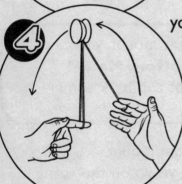

4. Make a circle with your yo-yo hand around the extended finger of your off hand, carrying the doubled string.

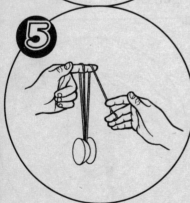

5. The yo-yo should land back in its starting position. This is called a front somersault.

6. To do a back somersault, you just reverse the motion. Push your yo-yo hand forward and back over your off-hand extended finger.

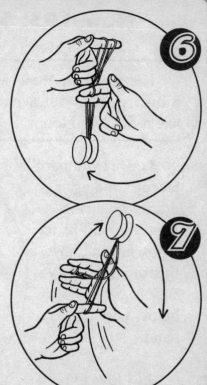

7. Push the string and yo-yo in a reverse circle around the off hand.

Let the yo-yo continue in the same direction for another circle off the string and back to the hand.

Hopefully, Brain Twister will apply only to your yo-yo and not to you!

Mount #5: Split Bottom

The **Split Bottom Mount** is a combination move. It starts out like a Front Mount but ends like a Bottom Mount.

1. Throw a hard Sleeper and again drape the string over your off-hand index finger. Only this time, the yo-yo should hang well below your yo-yo hand.

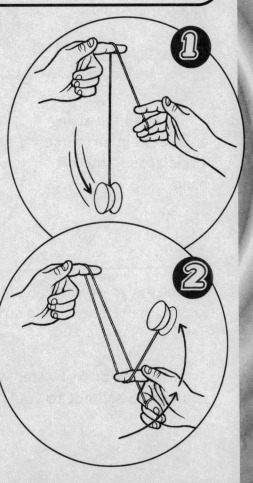

2. Now, extend the index finger of your yo-yo hand, and swing the yo-yo around that finger toward you. The yo-yo should loop over the index finger of your yo-yo hand, swinging front to back, just as in a bottom mount.

3. Land the yo-yo on the string farthest from you, so it ends up spinning within a loop of string.

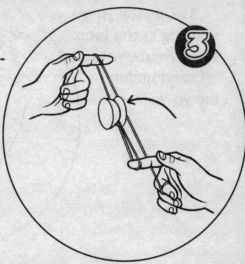

Use the Split Bottom Mount to do the **Front Barrel Roll**.

1. Get the yo-yo spinning in the loop. Then, rotate your off hand under the yo-yo.

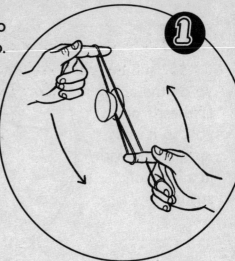

2. The index finger on your yo-yo hand follows in the same direction.

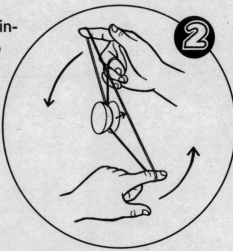

3. You're actually rolling your fingers so that the yo-yo passes from one string to another, inside the loop.

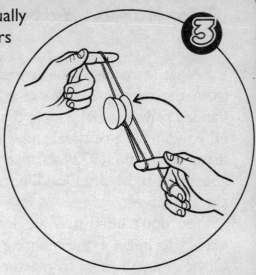

Two Hands: Better Than One?

What separates the expert yo-yo players from the merely excellent? It starts with two-handed play. A lot of people think that two-handed yo-yoing is a relatively new art. Not so. it was featured in the 1932 world championships and goes back to before Don Duncan got involved in the sport.

You don't need to wait until you're a yo-yo expert to begin experimenting with two yo-yos. Obviously, you need to master your main yo-yo hand — your dominant hand — first. That's what this book has been about — until now. When you feel comfortable with one hand, begin thinking about two-handed play.

Start working with your opposite hand. It's kind of like writing with your bad hand, so be patient and start with the simplest tricks. That means the Gravity Pull, the Power Throw, and the Forward Pass. Believe it or not, some excellent players end their two-handed careers right here. They're simply not capable of doing anything with their off hands.

According to Dale Oliver, you need to start your off-hand work with simple down-and-up moves, followed by loops. The objective in all yo-yoing is to do something perfectly once. After that, it's just a matter of doing it again and again. Can you do it perfectly twice? Three times?

Eventually, you'll get used to using your off hand in single yo-yo tricks and then you'll be on your way to the two-handed world! The key is to mirror with your off hand what your dominant hand does.

Your goal might be to learn to do a series of perfect Inside Loops with your off hand. How many can you get? Five? Ten? Twenty? If you can do twenty-five, you're well on your way to becoming a two-handed expert! How about Outside Loops?

And even when you master off-hand tricks, becoming a two-handed player takes time and lots of practice. Remember to be patient with yourself, especially at the beginning.

When you're ready to try two yo-yos together, try a **Two-Handed Sleeper**.

Then comes **Walking Two Dogs**.

Next, try a **Double Creeper.** All you have to do is throw two good Sleepers and Walk the Dog out in front of you. Squat down and give your yo-yos a jerk so they "creep" back to you on the ground.

Are you ready for **Double Loop the Loops**? If you can do Inside Loops with both hands at the same time, you're really rocking and rolling.

The double loops open up lots of possibilities. If you can get both yo-yos going out and coming back at the same time, you might try **Croᴀᴀing Loopᴀ**.

In this trick, the yo-yo strings cross each other on the trip out. This requires a huge amount of coordination! If you get it, try alternating crosses by having one yo-yo going out while the other is coming back. Talk about impressive!

Now it's time to combine loops in one hand and another trick in the other. Most of the top pros recommend doing the loops with your off hand while you perform the featured trick with your dominant hand.

You can, for instance, combine **Loops** and **Around the World**.

During your double loops, you can occasionally throw in an Around the World with either hand. You just continue to do double loops until you're ready to go Around the World.

Ready to Compete?

If you've gotten this far with a high degree of skill, you're ready for formal competition. The requirements vary according to your age and your experience.

The American Yo-Yo Association (AYYA) sets the regulations for most of the formal yo-yo contests, though the rules are fairly flexible.

For example, take the Beginner Division for kids 8 and under. The AYYA recommends these tricks for this group: Gravity Pull (dropped from a palm-down position), Forward Pass, and one Loop the Loop. That's it. But the AYYA also says these are just suggestions, not absolute rules.

It's the same in the Novice Divisions (12 and under, 13 and over). In many contests, you'll need to perform a two-second Sleeper, Forward Pass, Over the Falls, Breakaway, Walk the Dog (at least six inches), Rock the Baby (one full rock, back and forth), Around the World, and Loop the Loop (five times). If you and someone else are tied, you may be asked to do a Three-Leaf Clover, Hop the Fence (five times), the Man on the Flying Trapeze (flip overs allowed), and if necessary, a "loop off," until the tie is broken.

Oh, you're better than that? Actually, if you win a regional, state, or national novice contest, you must move up to the Advanced Division the following January 1. Advanced yo-yoers who are age 15 and younger compete in the Junior Division. If you're 16 or over, you're in the Senior Division.

Advanced competitors have to meet much higher standards. Some of these tricks are even too complicated to show in this book! Generally, advanced competitors need to complete the following tricks: Walk the Dog (one foot or more), Around the Corner (plucking the string with the yo-yo hand), Reach for the Moon (2 times), Three-Leaf Clover, Hop the Fence (10 repetitions), Skin the Cat or Tidal Wave, Rock the Baby (3 times), Sleeping Beauty, the Man on the Flying Trapeze (including flip overs if you wish), and Inside Loop the Loop (15 reps). If two competitors are tied, they go to sudden death, starting with a Brain Twister with one somersault. Next comes the Man on the Flying Trapeze with one somersault and no flip overs, followed by an Atom Smasher.

If you're a winner in the Advanced Division,

you move to the Expert Division. That's open to any yo-yoer, regardless of age. At national competitions, all of the sport's superstars are at this level.

The AYYA recommends that the following tricks be required in the Expert Division: Reach for the Moon (10 repetitions), Pinwheel (3 reps performed vertically with a pullover from a sleeper, finishing with an upward toss dismount), Planet Hop (10 reps), Brain Twister with two somersaults and a Skin the Cat dismount (no string hit misses), Punching Bag (10 reps), the Man on the Flying Trapeze with two somersaults and an upward toss dismount and no flip overs, Warp Drive (3 regenerations of Loop the Loop going on to an Around the World combination), Double or Nothing with an upward toss or rolling upward toss dismount and no flip overs, Time Warp (Forward Around the World punched to Backward Around the World), Atom Smasher (split bottom mount, completed with one somersault and a dismount with no flip overs or string hit misses).

The Association recommends breaking ties using freestyle tiebreakers or a sudden-death tiebreaker using a Warp Drive/Time Warp Combination, 20 Reach for the Moons, and 20

Planet Hops. Still tied? Move on to 40 of each of those tricks, and continue until the tie is broken.

The Expert Division Freestyle competition is a three-minute performance that can be part of the compulsories or a separate freestyle contest.

For world-class players, there's the Championship Division, which, like the Expert Division, has no age restrictions. In this division, the Association has compulsories for one yo-yo and for two yo-yos. Most of the tricks are done as they are in the Expert group.

Single yo-yo compulsories are: Reach for the Moon (25 reps), Punching Bag (15 reps), Warp Drive/Time Warp combo (3 regenerations), Atom Smasher, and Triple Trapeze.

Double yo-yo compulsories are: Loop the Loop/Crisscross Combinations (5 of each), Milk the Cow (10 reps), Ride the Horse (10 reps), Whirlwind (inside and outside Loop the Loop, 10 reps), Loop the Loop/Reach for the Moon (10 reps), Outside Crisscross (5 reps), Loop the Loop/Punching Bag (5 reps), Punching Bag (5 reps), Reach for the Moon (5 reps), and Cattle Crossing (5 reps).

A tiebreaker for Experts requires doubling the number of reps in each of the double yo-yo tricks until the tie is broken.

Because freestyle judging is so difficult, the AYYA recommends keeping the freestyle competition separate from the compulsories at this level.

Freestyle

When yo-yos first swept the nation in the 1930s, the Duncan Yo-Yo Company hired demonstrators to teach kids how to yo-yo. Today's sport is altogether different. And what separates the modern sport from the older version is freestyle.

What is yo-yo freestyle?

Think about gymnastics and figure skating. One of the reasons people flock to those sports in such huge numbers is the show. On top of the athletes' extraordinary strength, skill, and grace, they also perform for the crowd, wowing them with their musical routines. The audience quiets, the music begins, and the athlete swings into action. The activities on the mat or the ice are perfectly timed to the most exciting music. Little did Tchaikovsky and Beethoven realize that they would become such important members of the sports world. Gymnasts and skaters have captured everyone's imagination with their freestyle shows.

The same is true of yo-yo. A freestyle routine is a three-minute festival of yo. It can be scored separately or together with the compulsories.

Either way, it's a real test for the expert yo-yoer.

Freestyle actually began in 1992 when Dale Oliver organized the first modern world championships. Since then, significant gains have been made in freestyle. Some of the competitors still don't take the freestyle component of the competitions all that seriously. You can tell by their uninspired choice of music or their uncoordinated routines.

But the most serious contenders really prepare for the event. They choose their music very carefully. And their yo-yo tricks match the music note for note. The choice of music, by the way, varies enormously. At major competitions, you're liable to hear anything from the classics to rock to rap. The ever-growing group of outstanding Hawaiian players, led by 1998 national champ Alex Garcia, lean toward upbeat pop with a strong beat.

In addition to inspiring music and coordinated performances, the secret of success in freestyle is simple: The fewer times you catch the yo-yo and the more continuous the routine, the better. If you keep the yo-yo going for as much of the three minutes as possible, you will be scored higher. In other words, you must master both regeneration and continuous loop tricks if you want to succeed. These are the basic building blocks of freestyle.

One of the problems with freestyle is, of course, the judging. Almost all of freestyle scoring involves someone's opinion. That someone is the judge. And because judging is, by definition, somewhat subjective and open to personal opinion, it can get a little tricky.

In every official competition, the freestyler gets two scores, one for technical execution and one for performance style. In technical execution, judges look to see if the competitor attempted more difficult tricks. They also look for originality, transitions between tricks, and transitions from vertical to horizontal planes. Competitors automatically lose points for loss of control and subsequent restarts. Any loss of control means a two-point deduction, one point for the bobble and another for the restart.

In performance style, judges award up to ten points to each competitor. Competitors can earn as much as two points for costuming and staging and another two for choreography (if the performance matches the music). The other six points are awarded by the judges for such things as stage presence, showmanship, speed, control, elegance, grace, and flair. In the end, the judges' numbers are averaged together to find a winner.

The move to freestyle yo-yoing has changed the character of the sport. Today's young freestylers jump and dance around the stage with great energy. The older folks who took numerous yo-yo titles simply can't keep up anymore. So at least on the national and world levels, the game has become much more of a young person's sport!

Superstars of Yo

Lots of folks know the stories of sports immortals. They know that Michael Jordan was cut from his high school basketball team. They know that home-run king Mark McGwire can hardly see without his glasses or contacts. The yo-yo greats have interesting stories, too. Here's what we found out.

Alex Garcia

In 1998, at the age of 15, Hawaii's Alex Garcia won his first United States double-handed yo-yo championship. But what many people don't know is that Alex never touched a yo-yo until he was 12!

"My first yo-yo wasn't very good," says Alex. "But I quickly found out that I enjoyed playing with it."

And he was pretty good, too. Within a year, he had won several major local championships and was discovered by Alan Nagao of High Performance Kites. Nagao has helped several yo-yo superstars develop their talent. By the time he was 13, Alex began traveling to Japan with Nagao, giving yo-yo shows and demonstrations.

It wasn't Alex's first Asian visit. He was born in Singapore and didn't move to the United States until he was 6 or 7. "Fortunately, English is the dominant language in Singapore," says Alex. "That enabled me to adjust easily when we moved to Hawaii."

Japan remains one of Alex's favorite places. "The fans there really get into yo-yo," he says.

He made his 17th visit there in April 1999 for Yo-Yo Day, when an amazing 40,000 people gather every year to watch some of the world's best players. Among the other Americans on hand: world champ Jennifer Baybrook of Vermont and a pair of young Hawaiians, Alan Batangan, the 1998 Hawaii champion, and Alfred Pacheco. "I think that in the near future, Alan will be my toughest competition," says Alex.

Alex practices yo-yoing once or twice a week. He also enjoys Rollerblading and plays a little backyard basketball. He credits all-timer Dale Myrberg with teaching him two-handed yo-yoing. "He gave me a couple of Coca-Cola yo-yos to get me started," says Alex. Myrberg is one of his yo-yo heroes, along with Bill DeBoisblanc and Dennis McBride, two other all-time champions.

How does Alex learn new tricks? "Mainly

from watching other yo-yoers," he says. When he sees something he wants to know more about, he asks his competitors. And in the true spirit of yo, they always cooperate. Then Alex adds his own variations.

To put together a routine, Alex selects the tricks and music he wants to use, and choreographs his own dance steps. Then he goes out and wins another title!

Alex plans to go to college after his June 2001 graduation from Moanalua High School in Honolulu. "I still don't know what I'd like to study in college," he says. But with his stellar performance in the classroom — he has a 3.5 grade point average — he should succeed in just about anything he tries.

Captain Yo: Don Watson

Talk about the Comeback Player of the Year! Captain Yo, otherwise known as Don Watson, was retired from yo-yo for nearly 50 years. But when the modern yo-yo craze began, the great man was ready to return. Now, in his mid-70s, he's back in the world of yo, entertaining and teaching everyone in sight.

Captain Yo (he selected the name himself

from a long list of possibilities) grew up in New York City. In 1932, when he was 8, he got his first yo-yo — a 10-cent red-and-black Duncan beginner. It wouldn't sleep, but young Don got it to do several tricks.

"Remember, this was the time of the Great Depression," he says. "Hardly anyone had any money." Eventually he scraped together five nickels and upgraded to a Duncan tournament yo-yo. "It was a pretty big deal," he says.

By 1939, Don was winning neighborhood contests regularly. "I won a sweater with a Duncan champion's patch. That was great." But he peaked in 1940, capturing a five-city contest on the stage of the Freeport Theater on Long Island.

"I got lucky," he remembers. "It was a sudden-death tournament. If you missed one trick, you were out. But I got through all the tricks and then did more than a hundred consecutive loops. The prize was the greatest bicycle I'd ever seen. That was some prize for a street kid!"

Soon after, the United States entered World War II. "I joined the Army Air Force," says

Captain Yo, "and that was the end of my yo-yo career." More precisely, it was the end of his *first* yo-yo career.

"My kids tell me I used to demonstrate a few tricks for them when they were growing up," he says. "But I don't remember it."

Then, in 1988, 47 years after his last run of serious yo-yoing, Don Watson was sitting at home watching TV's *Smothers Brothers Anniversary Show*. On the screen, Tom Smothers was wowing the audience with his yo-yo tricks. But he also was reminding a 64-year-old man in northern California of his boyhood sport.

"I told myself that I could do all of those tricks. I was hooked instantly," says Don. Within days, he was in touch with Don Duncan, Jr., the son of the man who originally made yo-yo an American pastime. Don Watson became a yo-yo distributor, a yo-yo demonstrator, and a yo-yo teacher. He attended his first national championship at Chico, California, and has missed only one since then.

Folks come from everywhere to see Captain Yo do his thing. He performs at the weekly street fairs in Santa Rosa, California. And he does school shows as often as he can. "I really enjoy that," he says. "I start with history and safety, then continue with all of the basics, beginning with a simple down and up, which can be a tremendous stumbling block."

Watson even invented a unique piece of equipment, which he uses to conclude his shows. It's called Captain Yo's Awesome and Amazing Yo-Yo Launcher. "I throw a hard Sleeper, slip the yo-yo off my finger, and race it toward the launcher," he says. "The device pops the yo-yo into the air, and I catch it in my hat."

Sounds like Captain Yo is really enjoying him-self — and his rediscovered sport! If you want to write to him, he loves e-mail. His address: capt-nyo@sonic.net. And if you happen to be in California and see a license plate reading capt-nyo, be sure to wave to the driver. It's Don Watson!

Mr. Brain: Mike Caffrey

It's a good thing for yo-yo players that Mike Caffrey doesn't take no for an answer. Back in the early 1980s, when he invented the first yo-yo with a Brain, everyone told him it wouldn't work and wouldn't sell. Now, about a zillion yo-yos later, Mike's brainchild has revolutionized the yo-yo world.

As you may remember from Technically Speaking, a Brain yo-yo has a special clutch system that makes the yo-yo return automatically. It "knows" when the yo-yo has slept for long enough, so it catches the string and winds the yo-yo back up, all by itself.

Asthma, which wrecked Mike's athletic career, indirectly led him into the world of yo. "I couldn't play football or baseball or basketball," he recalls. "But when I saw one of the old-time Duncan demonstrators, Gus Somera, showing kids his yo-yo tricks at a hobby shop near my house, I figured here was one sport that I could really try."

Within a short time, Mike became the yo-yo king of his Tucson, Arizona, neighborhood. He and his brother Patrick were so good that when they showed up for local contests, the other kids stuck their yo-yos in their pockets and shuffled off. Eventually Mike himself began touring the country for Duncan, living the yo-yo life to the fullest. But he decided he should take his hobby in a different direction.

"While I was at the University of Arizona," he remembers, "I had a dream. After a little studying,

I realized that I could develop a yo-yo with a clutch that could sleep a lot longer than any fixed-axle yo-yo. I really believed it could change the sport for the better."

The start-up was a little difficult. The man he hired to design the prototype couldn't get the yo-yo to work. "Forget about it," the designer suggested. But Mike showed him how to make an adjustment, and the Brain did everything Mike hoped it would.

Marketing was still harder. When Mike brought his invention to his old company, Duncan, owner Bill Sauey advised him that the public simply wouldn't spend five bucks on a yo-yo. (In fact, when Mike's first yo-yo hit the market, it cost $10!) Fortunately, Mike didn't listen to Mr. Sauey, either.

He was granted a patent for his brainy toy in June 1982. With a little bit of luck, and funding from his new business partners, the Amaral family, Mike finally got the product off the ground. Mike and the Amarals started the Yomega Co. in 1984 and sold their first Yomega Brain in August 1985.

Yomega bought Mike out in 1987, licensing the patent from him. Since then, Mike has worked with a variety of companies with tremendous success at every stop, including stints at Duncan and with the promoter Alan Nagao, at Bandai. He is now the marketing manager for SuperYo, a Washington State company. You can reach them at www.tricks. yoyoplace.com.

Mike credits the recent American yo-yo explosion in part to a demonstration on *The Rosie O'Donnell Show* in 1997. "She had one of our young (age 11) superstars on the show," Mike recalls. "He had never seen a TV camera before — and he froze. Rosie jumped right in, easily performing all of the basic tricks —and a few harder ones, too. Within weeks, every yo-yo in retailers' stock was gone. There were hurry-up calls to most manufacturers for more product. It was incredible."

Mike doesn't play much yo-yo anymore. "I don't have time," he says. "I really like to design marketing programs. I've always been something of a tinkerer. If I played yo-yo six hours a day, I could never get my work done!" But he still demonstrates at trade shows and admits to being pretty good.

When asked to identify the world's greatest yo-yoer, Mike doesn't hesitate. "Until very recently," he says, "it was Dale Oliver. He was good, and he was a little wild. He was really exciting. But now, there's no question in my mind. Alex Garcia is number one. He has taken the sport to a new level."

So has Mike Caffrey's brainchild!

What's Next?

If you've gotten this far, chances are you're pretty serious about the sport of yo-yo. You've learned more than 30 tricks. You're probably playing with two yo-yos at a time. You've heard about the revolution of the 1990s, freestyle play. And you've gotten advice from some of the leaders, young and old, of the sport.

Maybe you can tell which yo-yos work best for you. And maybe you own several of the latest models.

Chances are, you're teaching your friends some of the tricks you've learned. That's what has helped yo-yo become such a popular sport. Remember what national champion Alex Garcia said about learning new tricks? When he sees another player performing a trick he'd like to learn, he asks for help.

So what's next? It figures that yo-yo will continue to grow as a sport. It's bigger and better than ever. Today's championship tournaments are attracting more players than they used to draw spectators. And the competition is fiercer than ever, too. Every superstar knows that somewhere in the world a new hopeful has the yo-yo championship in his or her sights. It's amazing how the sport has changed in the few years since the first modern world championships in 1992.

Yo-yos will continue to become even better, too. Designers all over the place are planning the next advance in the world of yo. I can't predict the technical changes — or I'd be designing yo-yos, too! Remember, however, that yo-yos have been around for thousands of years and most of the important changes have taken place in the last ten. So keep your eyes and ears open for the latest products.

The new art of freestyle will certainly develop, too. As recently as 1992, there was no such thing, since Dale Oliver created the style when he put on — and won — the first modern-era world championship. In just a few years, freestyle has made yo-yoing a more athletic sport than it has ever been. As a result, more and more titles are won by younger players. Teenagers, like Jennifer Baybrook and Alex Garcia, have moved to the top levels of yo-yo. And their biggest rivals are even younger players.

Finally, the next advance in the sport will probably come in "off-the-string" tricks. These are done by launching the yo-yo off the string and into the air, catching it back on the string, and performing a series of special tricks. Off-the-string moves are probably more difficult than anything we've seen up 'til now, simply because the yo-yo and the string are no longer attached. Dale Oliver gave me a personal demonstration one night. Seeing the yo-yo dents in his ceiling, I instantly knew how difficult it was to control the yo-yo's flight.

Meanwhile, you probably have enough to keep you busy for a while right here. Though Alex Garcia says he only practices a couple of days a week, it will take you a little longer to really master the tricks you've learned. Once you do, there's still a long way to go. It has been reported that Dale Oliver knows more than 200 tricks. But new moves are being developed all the time, particularly involving two yo-yos.

How do you keep up? You can check the various yo-yo newsletters, visit contests in your neighborhood, see if any of the yo-yo pros are giving a demonstration near you, or even plan a trip to the next U. S. championships. They're held every October in Chico, California. (Call 530-893-0545 for details.)

The Internet will give you even more information. The best advice: check your search engine and conduct a yo-yo search. Most of the yo-yo web sites are linked to one another. Oliver's site at www.Spintastics.com will give you information on Dale's new award patch program, which is already underway in the U. S. and Europe, among other places. The American Yo-Yo Association site, www.pd.net/yoyo, will give you the latest competition results and rules.

So enjoy the ride. Practice hard but have fun — which, after all, is what it's all about!